Mark Scroggins was born on a military base in Frankfurt am Main, and grew up in various places, relocating at drearily inevitable two-year intervals—West Germany, upstate New York, California, Texas, and Kentucky—and ultimately settling in Tennessee. He was educated at Virginia Tech and Cornell University, and now lives in south Florida, where he teaches and directs the graduate program in English at Florida Atlantic University. His previous books of poetry are *Anarchy* (Spuyten Duyvil, 2003) and *Torture Garden: Naked City Pastorelles* (Cultural Society, 2011). His *The Poem of a Life: A Biography of Louis Zukofsky* (Shoemaker & Hoard, 2007) was widely reviewed. He writes regularly on contemporary poetry for *Parnassus: Poetry in Review* and *Chicago Review*, and has published critical essays in a wide range of journals and collections.

Red Arcadia

Mark Scroggins

Shearsman Books

First published in the United Kingdom in 2012 by
Shearsman Books
50 Westons Hill Drive
Emersons Green
Bristol
BS16 7DF

Shearsman Books Ltd Registered Office
30–31 St. James Place, Mangotsfield, Bristol BS16 9JB
(this address not for correspondence)

http://www.shearsman.com/

ISBN 978-1-84861-192-4

Acknowledgements
Some of these poems have appeared in *The Cultural Society, Elixir,
Fascicle, FlashPoint, Intercapillary Space, Marsh Hawk Review,
Notre Dame Review* and *The Rumpus*.
My thanks to the editors.

Contents

I

II

III

For JL

I.

Dawn, New & Improved

Turn the sun rising into
a new genre, dubbed for want
of better words *solar apotheosis.*
Slug down the coin slot,
night down for blurred metal
racket, cat calling for her
husbands. Reach across her back
for the door lock, gear box
frozen and matted. As authoritative
as he may appear, suddenly
the sky cracks with motion—
women and men running, backpacks
purses briefcases scattered heedless before
the sun of a new
trademark. *Logos* as logo, descending
dove whose feathered breast touches
your lips for one aching
moment before the darkness falls
and endless credits scroll. I
am in a box somewhere,
beyond the rumblings and gurglings
of the tongueless dialectic, flicking
a lighter to make out
the cramped curves of my
own limbs, sapless. Someone planned
it all, brought us to
this sorry pass. Waves pink
far as the eye sees
under the tumid, bristling
orb—and a blanket crusted
with sand, rimed with salt.
You are in a box

somewhere, as Spirit unfolds itself
in the patter of dirt
and the thud of clods
drizzling down over your head.

Captain Modernism

The pictures no longer tell tales,
nor do the symphonies give us
Broadway themes. I took pleasure
in the woven plaits
of your sunshine locks, subservient
firms once again took them around
a back alley
for a thrashing.
I am beautiful, you
are sublime, the prettiest thing
ever seen since Mont Blanc,
where blue-eyed skiers slide
down diamonded inclines.
We want to know intimately
how it punches each of us
in sequence out
of the self-same metal
flimsy substance, or how the boys
with their tattoo'd backs
and shining mandibles
can seize so effectually
the days. Blue eyes, shining
teeth and fingernails,
frozen on the windowsill
that separates the revolving mind
and its noumenal,
untouchable object. Play it
again, watch the play count
rise and roll over.
Fido is faithful, and
a dog. His rites consist
of fleaing, fetching, scratching, donning

an ossuary chasuble—flicks drops
of water from the wafer, and drops it
onto waiting beaded tongues.
Confronted by the polished black
of the maze's wall, Captain Modernism
uses never before suspected super-powers, turns
back time
to where her rescuees find themselves
snuggled around the fire in bespoke
upholstery, brandies warm, cigar alight.
Like a picture, which no longer tells tales.

Flâneur

The commodity strolls through the shopping mall,
peers into each store, turns over
price tags, casts a cold eye
over advertised specials. In the movie

a four-thousand-years-dead Egyptian boy
finds his way to his parents—among
the stars—with the aid of a giant
yellow bird (species undetermined)

and a long-haired, tuskless dwarf
mastadon. There is a proper way
to turn these things inside out, unravelling
which no optical contrivance

can blacken or occlude. Sunset
lavenders spin their ways down
through a tall cool one, a hand-held
tracking shot that lingers on palms

and corrugated fences to beat back
the constant drumming traffic. Culling
over price tags and casting advertised
eyes on exposed breasts—the polished

leather, laced and tightened around
white-and-peach-fuzzed thighs, the pins
of heels and woven rattan mats, home.

Burano Lacework, Murano Glass

Eyes livid veined and water-streaked
stare at a tracework of threads and pins.
Observe, sir, this leaping world,
the slow leak in the convertible's
left rear tire, and consider
the strangeness of your circumstance.
The fires burned down
all evening, blackening walls
and ceilings, the dawn seeped through
in unexpected colors. The angle of incidence
and the angle of refraction, the recording
angel that walked with God, and was not,
are numerals fixed in the mind
then forgotten. With what system
did you produce these words, sir?
Or did the pencils move themselves
at your fingertips, limn the lines
and curves and limbs of your
greedy secret desire? That pink thing
(and here I point—*you*, sir)
struggling to raise itself from the carpet,
is that alone the sum of your fears
and hopes? He upheld it as though
it were hot, his hands weak, their blotches
spreading like a spilled beverage. It is easy,
she said, to lay a graceful period beside
another, string sentences on a wire
like stars of millefiori glass—Ruskin hated
those Venetian beads, drawn to a monotonous pitch
and clipped from careful fragile rods.

Connection Static

His steel-toed shoes setting
        off the airport's metal
detector, they took him aside
        to search him. The grass
was vivid across the pavements,
        the sky was lowering, dark.
Place, taken place, and token
        assignation. Slanted raindrops
cutting the plexiglass scratched.
        Moist light like an evening's
digital shift numerals careening
        through their base-ten cycles
and stars the Chrysler's windshield.
        His wife, the infant
in her arms, pregnancy fat
        still pillowed around her
ankles, would kiss his cheek
        as he threw his briefcase
onto the sofa. Birdsong,
        cricket-song, the restless
sounds of deep, unsubstantiated
        night, fell on the ears
of the child, bright-eyed
        at five months and some
days. An air-conditioned storage
        space full of furniture. Black-
eyed peas and green beans in
        Mason jars sweet corn blanched
and frozen. Some Theseus, Mycenaean
        super-hero, could do it, untangle
the twines of the varicolored
        paper kites the old man used

to fly in his vacant lot, behind
        the closed convenience store—dust
in the aisles, knotty plywood mending
        one spider-webbed plate-glass pane.
Searching him they found nothing.
        In the concourse, he could imagine
like a raptor's beak the airliner's
        shadow, cutting across
ponds and streams, breast
        of the Bovary husband reaching
up for the posthumous scalpel.

Papillon

Tattoos, pricked and chased, cunning
lines and multifoliate detail, scale
her arms, winding ladders or dancing
Maghrebi brides, black eyes gleaming
beneath the hennaed embroidery of scent-
thick hair. Daylight fallen face-down, stirring
only at the scratch of the intercom,
he pulls the sheets over an unwashed
head; and a weaving, noiseless buzz
rings between his ears. She switches on
the radio first thing, and it "plays"—
emits sound—the livelong day, even
when she says she's "thinking." Mr. Evan
Moonley, brushing his teeth, catches
the flash of silver from his tongue, the tang
of quicksilver from his fillings—alchemical
mortality. Tattoos—fading numerals braided
among the sparse hairs of slack, translucent
forearms—are rarer these days in the Diamond
District. A supper at the Hotel: heavy cloth
napkins, dimmed lights, lobster under
a silver dome, and the ambassador—making
his apologies—departed. Revealed in the tabloids,
after his shocking death, was the butterfly
tattoo his khakis always concealed, leaping
the Gap between celebrity and sailor.

Boo-boo

A porous membrane, swelling around
to welcome the intrusive object
and sketch in chalk basics
of the mechanisms of healing;
 pursues a love affair with the dressing,
 grasps and clings, osmotic
freeway swell salving dirt
into the weeping wound's lens;
 the species fumbles midway through
 a bad luck run no longer
 to be denied, but what possessed us
to make this stake on chance, unmarked
unexpected offramp where clouds scud
and swag, scab and dangle, grasping
and changing; the flag in the windshield
 is fidelity and petty love, a magnetic
 ribbon supporting overseas manufactories
 and the export of blood death thunder
 shock and awe; I am haunted
by images of dismemberment, evisceration,
wretchedness and deformity. Postmortem Edgar
Poe lies like an angel, skin clear and bright;
at that point the sky no longer browns
eagerly, creamy, but blotches in embarrassed
roseate patches, blobs of fractured melanin.

Dumbfoundry

Isn't it grand when the rumors
turn out to be *true*?
as the videos flicker
across the laptop, I reach out
and press my fingers
to the screen: blowtorch
that *steady, penetrating*
scrutiny of men and
affairs, while the wind
blows pixels of money
from hand to mouth, uncounted
accounts: we are bought
and sold through direct
deposits and mail-order
catalogues, but is
my price-tag showing?
Intelligence, said some
four-eyed elitist sod,
is a moral category: overworked
here in the dumbfoundry,
compulsory monogamy
goatfuct usufruct:
facing the future white-knuckled,
fanatical equanimity hanging out
the front of my trousers.

World Culture

The poem, someone quotes
        Mandelstam, speaks *nostalgia*
for world culture. Which rings true
        to shapeless intimations, cadences
forces welling up beneath the swells

        of centuries, coalescent imperial
cloudwalls, even scattering before theoretical
        winds, sympathetic tsunamis.
Nostalgia for a mythic unfallen, garden
        of single speech, singular ideographic

traced on the vibrating air; but what
        about *false* nostalgia, *nostos*
to a household where the traveler
        is as strange as
the swaggering salesmen drinking skins

        dry, summoning another fatted calf?
When I greet you lips to lips,
        is that osculation a posture of body
or society, a myriad of bodies
        jostling, penetrating, pressing

apart? Nature is after all culture,
        or springs from self-same
roots. I turn it over in my hands, a bit
        of soft marble coaxed and buffed
into the forms of the Blessed Virgin

and her canny son, one raised eyebrow
and blessing forefinger. This is or is not
            every mother, or some savage fetish
to trigger a thousand howling swords
            pillaging and sacking. Today, behind glass

in an endless phalanx of self-same
            burnished fetishes, fiery beneath
the stares of pressing crowds, she is world culture.
            Imaginary museum of ostended
nipples and actors' astral crowns.

Vasa Leviathan

Rain blankets and swathes us, the harbor's
        gorge rising to meet the leaden
sky, the mighty, hapless *Vasa* cabled up
meter by straining meter from what she thought
        a final rest; that ship heaves
        into view, barnacled
with bright carvings, polychrome, bristling
with Lutheran ordnance, national pride.

Awning tattered loose in the wind
        and rain; sunbeam marks a clot
        of albumenoid sperm, half-drying
on the tiles. Prosperity's banners frame
        a concomitant rise in "lifestyle"
        diseases, spotlit Mormon Tabernacle
card slipped into a first-grader's
lunchbag; the smear of banana; redolent
        moustache.

            The war is the crawl
        at the foot of the television
display, body counts ticked off
in pixels and automatic Nielsen
        Ratings. Precious fluids, congealing
        and refined, white as the gloves
on a lager heiress's pilot hands.
Belts and webbing bulge the prosthetic
        crotch.

        Ahoy for the cities of ferries
        and kayaks, waterways of Venice,
Stockholm, New Orleans, Amsterdam.

Aseptic Swedish beauty of straight lines
        and white spaces, blips
        of color punctuating the blank;
I hobble through the rain
on cobbled streets, lanes and closes
        rising up at outlandish angles
        from the puddled leaden
bay. The *Vasa*, dried and trimmed
and swallowed in gloom, haunts
        its vast interior. It waits
        to eat us all.

II

Goldfinches

I left the hospital and drove home in the rain,
windshield wipers beating out of sync
with the music the radio relayed. The very first
thing I remember is irrecoverable. For all their
advantages, electronic balance statements
demand the same expenditures of attention.
Take, for instance, those rolling briefcases—easier
surely on the back, but an inexplicable assault
on canons of taste, or bourgeois individualist
schemata of strength and self-reliance.
Experience fades from moment to moment, and leaves
no marks in the folds of my subjectivity.
The tragedy of grief is that I can no longer feel
grief, that my eyes roll like the earth's sphere
over words he scribbled in margins
and like the earth's sphere neither slow
nor stop. Goldfinches in the trees
indicate migratory season, and the increase
of nocturnal birdsong. Our avian
listening, infused with pleasure, bespeaks
a kindred echo perceived, the interpellation
of a *sensitive* ideal. The humanist
put down his pipe and scratched his beard,
composed a mordant footnote, only
to strike out half its words. "I've blacked out
twice today from the medication
for my mental illness and don't think
I should be driving." A closer examination
of premises, and failing that, the search team
should move on ("downward"?) through
layers of clammy, decaying, even verdant
self-deception: something will turn up in the end.
Many are sold, but the view is chosen.

Goldfinches

Were I involved in this matter
in any direct way, I would comment
on the medieval figure in its wizard hood,
the seeming caftan hanging below
its arms, the bare toes clutching
the tiny box, balancing for life, and the wires
that rhizome from the fingers, wryly unattached
to any power source. Tonight we missed the last
episode of *Friends*, and must bid farewell by proxy
to the fantasy of airy and affordable Manhattan
apartment space. In the labored sarcasm, the
unforeseen juxtaposition of planes and polished shadows,
the pointed periods, I feel rumbling in my bowels
the inner gears of the world's machinery,
the modes of production that produce the tree,
the true, the beautiful, the country and city,
nature, and you and me. A table of periodic
sentences. Landscape a painting behind sashed
glass. The air the men breathed, it has been estimated,
had by the third day circulated through
some two hundred pairs of lungs. Lunges.
A drop in tone, so I may speak in my own
voice, or one that bears the marks I associate
with me: Oh! for the carefree life of the pirate!
the salt spray humming in the rigging, the jolly
roger, flintlocks and cutlasses, buggery and bandanas!
Sing an accountancy chantey, ranking your debits
in one column, your credits in another, pierce
the mist of green trunks and feathered leaves
surrounding the glassed-in study, and grasp
the thing itself, the irreversible crawl of data
beneath the nipples of the bland announcer.

Watch the pretty newsreader take off her clothes
as she recites the headlines. "Supersize me,
baby," says Bob Dole. A series of tabular
definitions. Yellow birds make forays from the grapefruit
tree, and leathery men sell the *Homeless Voice*
at the light. My tongue in your ear is politics.
It is a beautiful thing, you know, a vast, all-encompassing
parent that gives and gives, eats and grows stronger
on whatever particolored, heterogeneous fare the streets
and hollers might evacuate onto its plate. A serious
deformation. My tongue in your rear is poetry.

Chicago
(for P. O'L. and E. M. S.)

1
a poem is crawling across the foot
of the screen, and a cursor
is erasing the words as soon
as they appear

2
crawling stock-tokens, and a man
furrows his brow to deform
a cliché, twist a platitude
into something approaching
rectitude, standing by one's word

3
four hundred channels buzz
revelation and midrash, rewording
the phone book's *sortes virgilianae*
in a colorized newsreel—the man
who pressed his cheek to mine, the woman
who kissed my throat on the darkened
dancefloor, have been digitally
removed—fallen under official
disfavor

4
like literal-minded Church Fathers,
their sentences—it is said—emasculated
themselves, a wallow of present-
tense verbs, passive copulatives

5

he died with the last stroke, last
poems scrawled or typed on pages colored
with coffee stains, wine rings, intravenous
drips—life encompassed in eight
acid-free cardboard document containers

6

she covered carefully the stroller,
with a blanket, before crossing the street—
a driving snow, pools of slush, honking
and snarling, a city a system
of alleyways and hardwood floors

7

pulsing joint of duck that melts
the camembert into the bed of lentil,
my fifth glass of wine, and money
throbbing through the muffled black veins
of the avant-garde

8

grace before challah, and the lighting
of the candles; on this day the LORD rested,
the ass rested, the manservant and the
maidservant rested, and the poets read

Mystic Seaport

Over some silent footage from the turn
of the last century, Ishmael
narrates the industrial techniques
of drawing forth Leviathan: cinematically
sterilized, the buckets of blood
rendered a grey-black celluloid
shimmer, the work of the precise,
wooden, floating abattoir before me
(for the first time) in living motion
echoes in dull but vivid *déjà vu*
on the video screen. Too neat:
fifteen, twenty chapters of viscous
dissection tried-out to six
minutes of jerky motion: the Book
of Job in *Reader's Digest* condensation.

Contrafactual

Hang it right there, beside
The case of striated, alcohol-
Swimming salamanders, or prop it
On the floor back of where
The door opens. Cream
        and brandy in my coffee

Blot out the sweet
Potatoes' peppercorns; at least
We're sitting at the grown-ups'
Table after all these years.
On the television the president's
        features seem pressed to

The center of his weasel-like
Face, little lips working
Like an asshole making buttons.
She can read at three, but
Are her ball-handling skills
        up to par? With so much

At stake or up for sale
How did you manage to choose
the *ugliest* sheep in the whole
damned flock? Striated like
Jacob's genetic engineering,
        the patriarch as science-

Fiction con-man. He loved
Her for her beauty, but the
Sister had weak eyes—the better
Not to be seen. Take me back
To Chicagoland, I beg of you,
        for it's there I feel

At home. The atmosphere's
A burden at best—though a thinner
Air would leave us panting
In our trousers. Lining up
For the big discount or
          the new release. I've not

Read his book, but I saw
The trailer, mysterious lines
Of semi-legible script
(Font "Cézanne") furrowing the walls
Of a *Pym*-like cavern. Wrote
          an opera called "The Treasure

Of Injun Joe." Rub my stickers
Off, nudnick! La vida es
Sueño, es verdad, but is it yours
Or the Red King's? Sullen
Gear-teeth ignite the pommel
          and thrust, trust in deity

Or currency, the bystanders
Stood by and the spectators
Looked on, but don't expect
Internal Revenue just to *listen*
At your audit. Sunk tho
          he be, watry floor or glass

Ceiling. Shocking white and black
Striations through the marble,
Courthouse like a quaking
Unsupported blancmange.
The painting—all dribbles
          and silkscreen—rubs history

Against the grain, gives a
Negative vision—black
For white, white black, etc.—
Of the utopia none of us
Will ever know; and it moves
        in the body, clicking

Of the eyes' valves
As they skibble over
The cracked and varnished
Surface. Under my palm
I felt the soft erectile
        hairs of your haunch, tremor

Of blood venturing and
Returning. The entropy
We chew and swallow defines
Itself in heat, in noise,
In chemistry, until it sinks
        to a level of common

Exhaustion, homogeneity.
With so much up for sale
And the currency's paper
Pinking like rosy-fingered
Dawn. Striations of light
        and Angel of God

Wields a pencil and brush
To scrub out the last two
centuries' errors. Draw me
A river, I'll draw an ocean
Over you. But truth—
        to principles, appearances—

Remains the establishment
Of his value. Affecting
The ancients, who told us
Lies and gross calumnies.
Scamper, huddle through the
        rain of contumely,

The bitter cup of realism. Curly-
Tailed lizards move south.
Sky-vine like kudzu, who takes
No prisoners. His hands striated
With paint and masking tape,
        he would gentle the child

As something precious. No-one
Gets out of here alive (quoting
Hank Williams), and if she wants
To be an Indian Princess, who's
To gainsay her? Like losing,
        sinking is an art

To which we're deeply apprenticed.
A dormitory bathroom, a semi-private
Hospital room, the cold comfort
And ambiguous hospitality
Of someone else's borrowed
        office, unofficially lent.

Measure twice, hammer once. Don't
Stumble over whatever's stacked
Around the pilings. Hunt out
What's lost—better yet, keep
Track of your heart's tchotchkes
        in the first bloody place.

Untitled

The spillage of sunlight into
    the still bowl of a windless
afternoon, humming with insects
    and a distant, unidentifiable
clatter. Something comes next,
    follows on. Time's logic, coded
in our very synapses, demands it.
    Spillage of sunlight into a
bowl of windless—but for a small
    breeze—afternoon. Flowers
purple, blue, bricks bleached grey
    and tan. Spillways of
attention, never settled or direct.
    Enter SECOND ACTOR, tottering
on chopines, face a horrified mask.
SECOND ACTOR: (*strikes pose, right hand on breast,*
    left hand outstretched, chest heaving magnificently)
    (*beat*)
Exit SECOND ACTOR. I sold my vote,
    recalled the old man, in the election
bazaar. For a handful of magic beans
    or a mess of red pottage. Spilled
like ochre cat-sick
    on the hem
        of the histrion's
chalked-white
    toga.

Untitled

But what was the question? I didn't think
we heard it all over the loudspeaker, the
morning announcements padded between
"Rapper's Delight" and "Free Bird," and you
with your head down in home room
on a stack of grubby books. Oh no,
it's new all right, fresh off the rack
with the tags still attached.

Listening to yet another man read something
vaguely from a sheaf of printout, we knew
this wasn't for us. Far better the brusque and gay
life of the entrepreneur, selling and buying
and getting laid.

It thinks in me. I cannot resist it. As if all
our darting attentions were waterbugs on
 a stream of commodities, channel-switching
infomercials for rubber band body-building
machines and alarmingly cute ceramic
animals. *It thinks in me.* Like yesterday's
sirloin on its peristaltic odyssey.

That machine grinds loud again. And it
was cold last night—I wanted a set
of fingerless Fagin-gloves to sit and scribble
in. A vacuum leak will keep the car
from starting dependably. Occult technology, as good
as magic.

Bathing in sun and air, wind over
limbs, wind-chimes competing
with the earbuds' cacophony,

it's not at all hard to feel exchange-
value licking at the pores
of the body (of course we do not enjoy
what we do not understand)—

the common life, continuous curve
of images cast onto our
sensoria, from dawn's electronic
chirp to the flaking scalp's
settling into a dented pillow. In the bath
of air and sparkling
water a voice sounds blown
over unseen ripples, dark waves
sirens calling out emergency or crowd
control trundle down pavements
the sun massages, strokes
and crumbles.

Untitled

Ask not reason, Klytaemnestra, or probe
       your ice-pick through those multiplying
diptych grams. Ablutions rain down
          worthy patronness, the saint
between cleric and layman gesturing
           prosperity and war. Black lines
       border yellow, red and the white
poofy quiff tangles in a down-heaving
       brand. Shave me clean as an ice-
pick, pink soft fasten bulbous. Splooge
         mascara no good for eyes um.

Caractacus shook off his chains temple
       trembling in wooden blocks—lintel
       pillars architrave and pediment—a sauce
         of pureed white beans garlic
       pepper salt staining blue cobalt plate.
A stiff January wind whips the page from the
       reader's hand, blurs over the
       microphones. I do not speak this language
well. I cannot read this second term.

       Spencer trends Dylan Andy Big Boy
       tangles of Nereia's hair not sandy
and in my mouth. A cowlick consummation
       tottering over the steps and into
        the bricks, brought them all
to what they assumed were their feet.
Vagueness, said Dr. R——, is the upright man's answer
       to the arrows and slings of outraged
       specificity. Pull me down another Meister-
brau. Pull out before you do it.

I do not speak this language term. Soft fasten
pulp prosperity war. Mr. Cleric, Mr. Layman, name
a "Chaplin" for the Aryan nation. Beat them
with baseball bats and feed their
texts or bodies through a shredder. I acted
only under orders, your honor, I did
chains temple bricks and feet of clay.
Too many deictics neuters and feminine rhymes
for this to be an American sonnet. Free to starve
to kill to speak someone else's mind.

My name is datum, my nature is
a gift. Oriel of oriole orisons sea
to shining scent, purged of scenic estuaries
methodical fjords and transient
sporting utility vehicles. My name is torture,
the best penetrant your money
can buy. A flag in every classroom, boiled
head in every pot: your sparrows
are numbered, ticked them off on nine
curled fingers and a twinkle toe.

Pull out before you do it, make sure the camera
has a clear shot. Money in the bank. *For*
casualties *read* casual tears, *for* remorse *read*
remoras, *for* regrettable errors *read* triumphant new
era. Galley proof slaves. Resentment
spawned a bright and shining obsession, poising
thought
against the blurred third-hand idea: *truth* is to
beauty as *duck* is to *rabbit*. Quack quack, said the
poet, which echoed through the fish-houses.

The full monty, as if talk
of sexuality would not seem objectionable

to someone, somewhere. Tie that one down before
it blows away. Guttural sound in the throat
    of the saxophone, scratched my leg
    on chemically treated mulch.
   Dragonfly, damselfly, ladybug, mosquito,
   a fog of bugs smeared across the wind-
shield. The word made flesh less interesting
   than its neon-bordered converse.

"Winsome" one of those looks to muster while
    sucking a finger and spreading it wide
   for the camera. Motion option
    whoreson poise. Beef and kidneys,
    liver lights and complicated
   closely packed flesh seins forward
   over time, as if time would make it all
clear, the rough places straight and the high
   places flat and easy.

I did not know what the word "anachronism"
   meant until you explained it to me.
   Eat your cellphone. A-1 vegetarian.
    A charming plastic pink house
   with a charming plastic blue roof, bleaching
in the sun, formalizes the informal garden, draws
   palms bushes ornamentals and sickly
grapefruit into an enlightened whole. Sedentary
   or sedimentary feet up and drawers down.

   Somewhere they're giving up the search
for chemical depots or stockpiled pikes and
halberds. Somewhere the clouds have squatted
   down over our heads like a corpulent ploughman
   taking a midday dump. Like, really,
   no kidding, man? The gear and wheels

are binding in an alarming mechanical
        obligato. Humming in my ears. And so
are we who are astonished to be loved.
Put it in park to remove the key.

        This one runs like a scalded
dawg! but the heat will bake your brains
right in your head. Don't sit there, Margaret,
        if you want to pee go back to your
        own damned room. Cash or checks
only No Credit cards No Debit. And bake
        the green out of those beans
        on the steam table. If you bread
        and fry it, he'll eat the sole
of a fucking shoe. And ask for seconds.

They grumble in the line at the deli counter:
        one half-pound of smoked turkey—*smoked*,
        you whoreson knave! No chance
        of a revolution happening here,
        and when it does we'll stay out
of its way. Smeared gravel and asphalt.
        Yesterday pink (the dead possum) today
        a stomach-turning pinky-
grey. Dodge the lightning bolts falling
        like pitchforks from a sun-powdered
        sky. Not *my* president baseball cap.

        A lizard straddles the pool fence, leaps
up to a post like a gymnast to the
        horse, reading between the lines of a
        newspaper three days out of date,
        waving another car into line with
        a gesture of two tobacco-spotted
fingers. If I knew anything about music, I might

understand Webern's reliance on voice
and texts, poems and singers. You can sing
anything to the tune of "Jingle Bells"
      and it sounds like the National Anthem.

      Once upon a time there
    was nothing here but swamp
    lizards and mosquitos but now
there's a solid chunk of concrete
      asphalt and fifty-seven
    varieties of ersatz. Choose your
ersatz carefully. One national anthem
    swaps with another, and who knows
      what that bald boy's singing there
in Arabic—I don't trust him.

Kassandra walks the battlements, chiton-
    hems blowing around her ankles. Turn, twist,
    dip and seize, make an answering harmony
      to the throbbing of that electrified
    intermittently seized-up pump. Tanglewoods.
    Black sails on the horizon. Red
sails. Assisted living and nursing home
care two separately defined spheres, where the
      cat limps along the fence,
    shunning the neighbor's animals.

Of Systems Subject, Political, and Private

One is thinking this morning
of revolution and despotism, faltering
hands at the dashboard of an immensely
large, immensely clumsy wheeled
machine. Watching the old men
cross the parking lot to the supermarket
in an ecstatic slow-motion, as if
the electric doors will slide open
on the riches of Ali Baba's cave.
Winding down towards the sleep
of stones in a perpetually more
quiescent rhythm, missing beats
and dropped feet. The sky
conjures motion from the black
fringes of trees, viral birdsong
downloaded on our heads
willy-nilly. Inference above
language, intuition of the divine—
perfect bullshit, at least to nodding cynics
who know that language hems in
our brains like a barbed-wire
fence. The world, Mr. Bronk—I say
gaily—is solid as you want it.

§

We make our own reality. We speak
a goodly frame, and the squamous facts
conform themselves thereto. At least that's
the official line. The end of history,
triumphal apotheosis of the behemoth
Capital, has been momentarily postponed.

§

Once upon a time Reason, or a deity,
extended itself and grew into the shape
of history. Once there was a "tendency"
in human affairs. As we buy
our shoes, lace them up, walk
our errands across the steaming asphalt.
Kiss our lovers or children, ignore
or huddle down against
the unspecified hour. Our present
swallows all pasts into its self-contented,
pixellated maw. The future,
a child screaming for your
admiration, is uncontained.

§

The Emerald City, the Rock Candy
Mountain, were levelled long ago
by the bulldozers and wrecking balls
of incessant imagination. You speak
of happiness in mutual labor,
a bright future of shared
sunrises and common weal—
I'm imagining you in a thong
and garter belt. The Paris Hilton,
I believe, was once only a hotel.

§

Lexus lanes arouse our virtuous
class indignation, but when haven't
we paid more coin to get there
faster? *Shanks's pony* a phrase

in need of annotation, like Ruskin's
illth, Hobbes's *state of nature*,
Pound's *usura*, Milton's *free will*.
Those exquisite polychrome tags
lighting up the railroad bridges—
Mr. Bennett, Mr. Bloom—
are scribbles in the margin
of Capital's black-letter folio text.

§

A certain sort of poet
would wind it all up
with a brisk *nostos*, renewing
Nestea plunge into the immediate—
the sun, unblurred by smog;
breeze unsmudged by particulate
from the abattoir or freeway;
a wee bit of cozy love, unconditioned
by the constant rain of copulation-
ready limbs on the plasma screen,
of printer-ready, skin-severing
admonitions and laws.

§

What we owe power, built
up in the telling, letter by
littoral, hands in the till
and finger-smudges smeared
on the edges of paychecks.
Dynamic, Greekly energetic,
power seizes us beyond intertia
and places us where it pleases;
diaphanous ridges smother

our eyes, waves edge over
our mouths to still
the crying.

§

The fine worked gold is hid
in a smudge of oily smoke.
Chances are few, but dance
and dance again, fuelled
by a kind of passionate
disinterest. Dance hard enough,
we'll disinter some ghosts
of old and hidden gain,
intricate dream-work's
final mouthless sculpture,
gaunt and cockless herm.

III

Lazarus

The train passing before us might well
explode in mid-tunnel, spending sharp
metal into walls, blowing clothes
off passengers to leave them naked,
charred, & bloody. Palm sheds its fronds
in the heat, bathtime emoluments.
The story hour ceased at the buzzer,
book half unread, with a smear
of fluorescent red paint like a bruise
beneath her right eye. Midway between
Independence and Bastille Days,
ancient regimes and upstart empires
tottering. "Due to the Jewish Holidays,
The Fall of the Roman Empire Will
Be Cancelled." Atheism no bar
to religious bigotry. The lunacy
that presses into conversation, barely
detained by cancellation and a bruise
beneath the eye. Storytime at bath
& buzzer, the train hurls itself
off the trestle into a ravine
where red-hatted gnomes dance
& smoke & count the dead.

•

He steps from the tunnel wrapped
in foulard ties and cerements, brown
with dried and crusted blood. She unwraps
tenderly his face, peeling the linen
from the cracks in his lips. We asked
you to dance, but you played no tunes.

Standing shin-deep in the river,
the vocables of emulation and praise
no longer sound, afford no further
ford or crossing. One way
or another, the gauges and meters
of baroque control panels, semi-
detachment and disarranged maturity.
We step out of the grave in ragged
winding sheets, trailing streamers of
glory; remember another life, but
that was another country, and wrong
life cannot be rightly lived.

·

The tides of affect
wash out and in, vary
   their formal intensities
with the dates of quotidien
consumption. Its imbricated clay
armor decayed and opening,
ornament paper saturates
   and makes a home
for earth-covering rain.
   Or it doesn't rain at all,
the sun bakes our brains in
their skulls, crying *Salt us! salt
   us! Milk for the mourning
cakes!*

·

Glass-framed skiey dome benath which
a woman of vines twists & turns & rubs
herself against the lamp-posts. Waves of

insect buzz & chatter as the fiduciary
breeze shifts, muddy heat crowding
in the attic's corners. Plastic toy
  soldiers outlast their regimes.
We drove in & out of the gulleys, patiently
expunging subjectivity from our letters
  & cards. The signs are turned
& rusted, fitted together with weakly
soldered conjunctions. Rain washes
  the black ink into a smear
of blue & yellow, the blue into
a skiey shadow.

Richard Kern

Mind you to remember is to put
        together what unhappy history has
dis-membered gathering the members
        of outsized outlandish Osiris

take them by regulation measured
        dosage and call out in the morning
the light reflected off their leaves
        and water-spangled branches the

highlights photoshopped onto that model's
        canines and bicuspids moist white
nights of sleeplessness rambling down
        and up blind flights of stairs

twine the ways apart my lord
        cleave backages and ransom
implements to filthy humus
        I for an eye truth for the

thunder and the lightning-
        bug sleepless the evil dead maunder
through an outlet mall of children's
        fancies outsourcing nail set

past a laboring proletariat switching
        channels swiftly as their thumbs
can twitch I had hope when
        violence was ceas'd handing

paper sovereignty to pasteboard
        crowns and lath scepters pat

buchanan my jo have all
          the seas ganged dry love of

lurchers sniffing sheeps' peeled
          hindquarters ye lightnings ye
thunders in clouds are ye come
          off the quaint pronouns mate

write something you could actually say
          in some emotion's stress or storm
our latest gesture neither an opened hand
          nor pointing finger but an odd

thumb-thrusting half-fist oh no he's
          not quite *fisting* her it's only three
fingers maybe the thumb so hard
          to see on that grainy super-8 stock

pay it no mind unless it's somehow
          marked folly magenta friendly
to unburthen one's self-same interior
          frames to hesitate out on a progress

whose time-stamped facets might imprint
          a passage pale indigent or parsimonious
a new atom mine where naked children
          haul coal-carts of glimmer and what's

the proper term for oral sex with the
          dead who can't really *give*
anything your handshake like a defunct
          fish cher monsieur bush good

thing the storm shutters're up early
          no she didn't pick up what don't

you screen your calls too incommunicado
        the chocolate flesh tones built up

by a dozen or more painstaking trans-
        parent layers of wash an icy
speaking warmth dream or nightmare
        of the moving statue *goylem*

soil 'em goylem roil 'em an aleph
        bracketed with the doubled horns
of the phoenician ox double ax
        of ariadne's maze a jackhouse

that jury built monument to the ten
        words break two tablets call me
deep in mourning a barbeque of aureate
        veal lechon asado chimichurri

vindaloo nouveau beaujolais rising
        up like the sun which is we are
told new each day they leaven the end-
        less parade of bleached teeth

and boob jobs with photos of a girl
        got her face burned off in a wild-
fire *true life human interest* florida
        scum on the white house train

eat or be what you eat testosterone
        panic button photosynthesize petrol
for a hybrid half-human half-turnip
        driver line up your fucking kids

and I'll run 'em down right now a bad
        hair life a tenderness in the angle

of her hand as she raised the cup
    to the old man's lips charity shines

in our leader's close-set eyes so
    careful not to soil them with
printed materials the charred face
    grins lipless over the lip of the

armored personnel carrier's turret compressing
    time and space in swift apery of far-flung
instantaneous markets electronic chads well-hung
    blond and toothy I'll bet wink and

bulge but why don't any of our letters
    get answered in characters we
recognize lovers' hands lapped in bonds
    of gold outcomes foreseen and outcomes

manipulated lie down take two
    alternatives implausibly standing in for white
and black odysseus's scar displayed and spread
    onscreen as just another weeping carnal gash.

Oliver Cromwell
(for Steven Moore)

He read of children tossed
at a pike's end, of cannons
with "God Is Love" scribed round
their barrels. He read of a snake
with garnet eyes, of golden
ringlets curling round the hemp
of a hangman's noose.
He read of green fields
and mines, of foundries
and factory floors. Pleasures
and game diversions. The tree
which bursts into pink blossoms
of enthusiasm. The trees huddle
suspiciously in the wind, rustle
in green whispers. A village mashed
and shattered under the sun, not one
stone left upon another. Bombers
and fighter jets darkening the sun,
the shop clerk whose weekend sends
him—in militiaman's uniform—
to take stock—with a bayonet—of a
tentful of refugees. Great men,
whose brows line with the effort
of shaping destiny. Who read old books,
and find their faces there.

John Milton Blues

I would have you take my words
as deadpan ventriloquy, take
them seriously indeed but not
as mine. (*The movie may be better—*
perhaps you should wait?) When eyes
swivel abject and aimlessly, to *see*
is metaphorical. The cap turned
backwards gives a clearer line
of sight, or fire, a rakish intellectual
look. Begin here, with the Argument.

§

Felix culpa, that original couple's
fuck-up redeemed in two books
of technicolor DeMillean flash-forward.
Old Sarpint at heel. A pretty story,
shot through with flashes of inconsistency
when Blind Pew's textual fidelity
scrapes against his flagging
narrative sense. We can't change
the ending, let's color outside the lines.
Make her face and nipples deep magenta.

§

Finding it hard to take *obedience*
as virtue, *nicht wahr?* Clever
classless and free, but nicer
in the end to be Napster's microserfs.
Twenty-first-century forecasts bullish
on air conditioning concerns, seawalls,

Kabbalah Energy Drink (*En soph*
perpetual source of profit and
enlightenment). Insurance payouts
on the rise. Best investment New Laputa.

§

The double skronk of the emergency
alert system interrupts the vicar-
author's interview, always. (*Just
kidding, folks!*) I would speak to you
of something important, tell you things
of great moment, could I disentangle
the kinks of these gags
and blindfolds. Dogs chawed
at my heels in the supermarket.
Voice from a speaker / voice of God.

§

A portable public address system,
handy for buskers or sidewalk
preachers. On sale now.
We condense our attention to one
harangue out of the Gomorran
clamor, as if probity singled itself
out more efficiently than cant,
counterfeited its placid façade
in waxless sincerity. What whiteness,
what candor—very like a whale.

§

Doctrinal and exemplary to reform
a nation, which supposes a nation

already taken form. Hard pressed,
imaginary auditors, to make something
of this shapeless mass. We can't
change the country, let's change
the channel. TIVO through
the commercial breaks, by all
means—I can't eat
what they're selling.

§

The big unscripted monologue
spirals away, spreads out
in pools and eddies like the crud
in Uncle Walt's beard, sleep-dirt
at the corner of Auntie Emily's
eyes. Another one. Tell us another
one, this time with a punchline
that'll make us laugh, sigh,
moan thoughtfully. Love's
old sweet frigging song.

§

Love's old sweet hands
on the wheel, like in the old
days—no question who wore
the pants, whose skirt got flipped
up around her hips at the drop
of an eyelash. *Subjection*
a non-starter *this* century, thank
God. We'll all bending over
to Nike, fumbling the nightstand
for the KY.

§

To *Columbine*, verb transitive.
I took off a-running. There was bullets
whizzing around my head. I didn't
see him good, but he looked foreign.
The smell, the light, the curve
of a place inhere in memory
like lines inhere around the eyes,
spots on the hands. I remember
how I stumbled on those steps, but never
fell, mouth salty with blood and cinders.

§

If Quentin Tarantino had wrote this,
the Liberals would say it's brilliant.
Say it, lone gunman, no ideas but—
or rather (to keep it simple) no
ideas period. A pose straight out
of *Scarface* or a Yakuza epic.
They'll love it down in Salem,
Christiansburg, Bluefield, the Christmas
tree farms of Floyd county,
out on the mush-trodden drillfield.

§

Astonishing how the world goes on
killing itself, cutting off bits
of its own body to roast
or eat raw and bleeding—while you
and I count the hours
of interminable Sunday afternoons,
lazy heat trapped beneath a bubble

of bürgerlich static contentment.
Almost a week since the last
disaster, greyed in the news cycle.

§

Astonishing, old lad, our universal
library, flickering up and erect
at the touch of a switch: wisdom
of the ages with constant updates
at a nominal fee. No more treble
voices halting through the Talmud
or Koheleth, mistaking vowel
pointing, ballocksing an aspirate.
Get a job, girls! Put those bitches
out to pasture.

§

Of all those boxes that tumble
through the mail to our doorstep,
which will explode between our opening
hands? What do the satellites
see as they peer down into our
backyards? My freedom stretches
only to the doorstep of your
safety—so they keep telling me.
Free will one word or two?
Sidereal paradise, slot loss.

§

The stars tell us, in daily doses,
that we are who we imagine ourselves
to be. Let me begin here, under

an auspicious sign: double-slashed
American dollar. Cynicism taken
too far threads one into the labyrinth
of self-conscious nihilism, fancy-free
anomie. Lone gunman, unspeaking
patron saint of quiet boys
on the fringe of the crowd, unspeaking.

§

All the cycles and happy ceremonies—
the balloon man, the face painter,
bounce house and cartoon cake—
are a blank to the speechless boy
growing up behind the dry cleaners,
drinking chemical fumes with his milk
and tasteless cereal. Six pages to describe
the careful consumption of whole milk—
frigid—and jagged Cap'n Crunch:
my staple in the Blacksburg dining halls.

§

Heat like prosperity, air-bath
inviting you to wander the back garden
naked, dabble the pool, settle into
a familiar lethargy of books and
papers where your only anxiety
is where to put the *stuff*—amnesia,
psychosis. Web-entangled, nexus
of discourses and memory, pushing
at every turn at the cling-wrap—
transparent, shimmering—of capital.

§

Was there in an uplift in that slow
rising bowl of green hills fading
into blue distance, from the airport
down the freeway to that brick house
staggered on its hill? Dusty rooms
of magazines, books, unremembered
knicknacks. Her presence everywhere,
whose flesh moves only around the wall
of a single room, eight times clockwise
in a treeless pavement sun.

§

The world winds down in a closer
and closer circuit, until the two
little girls walking a clockwise
revolution around the sun
are stepping on one another's
heels, turning back to back
and tangling their four braids together.
Playing at aging. To hasten
what one would fight, circum-
vent, resist at any cost.

§

We turn, arms stretched out, and try
to grasp the whole which cannot
be grasped. See the fibers and pores
of a patch of its skin, deduce
the workings of one bit machinery
or the hinge of a minor joint.
cities are thus built, or thus, let
me rather say, clotted and coagulated...

casting out the scum and scurf of them
into an encircling eruption of shame . . .

§

No one walks these crusty, humid
streets, sun-baked, gasoline-stained,
by choice. Forget the joy of shooting
the car's wheels through vast puddles,
watching tattoos bleach to grey
under a baking sun. Scabs
of gas stations, convenience stores,
scurf of strip malls and endless
office space, houses cloned and huddled
behind card-keyed gates.

§

The mind wiped clean, new marks
upon it fading as soon as they appear—
only rancor remains, resentment
and anger, like the second-hand
resentment of a people whose grand-
parents have been dispossessed,
who grouse and murmur, longing
for the tiled porches of splendid
houses they have never seen, shining
blue pools and gleaming appliances.

§

Grit my teeth to see old age
tottering along the gangway, one hand
outstretched as if to catch a missing
railing. Gnash teeth at spiderwebs

and moldy caulking, write checks
to open up hair- and shit-clogged
sewer lines. The skies are blue and hot
at mid-day, deliciously crisp
in the morning. Hills, hills to feed
hill-dwellers' passionate insularity.

§

Beat it down and it still
comes back green as ever. Country
of origin for this meat is uncertain.
Small libidinal economies, micro-
loans of passion—poetry as history
of affect, squeezed between
Benneton ads and wry cartoons.
Praise the Lord, I've been redeemed
like a coupon at the Payless
on double-coupon day.

§

The difference lies between *pardon*
and *commutation*, no? and one
must gravely admit one's sins
at best have been passed
over, overlooked, looked over, mis-
laid: but not *pardoned*, no.
My faults and failings pursue me at night
like the tin can tied to the cat's tail.
One sifts the till, making sure all George
Washington's heads glare in the same direction.

John Milton Blues

Tumid boughs weigh the fruits,
split with impact on the bricks
below. Purple blown flowers

moved between the wind, with the moistness
of yesternight's rain. Nightmare, which
bunged a year's anxieties

into a half-hour of staring fright:
connections lost, distance
uncovered, ignored responsibilities:

glossy magazine lineup of imploring
harelipped children. The war
drones on in the background like

an ill-fitting clock. Morning
would diffuse light into leaves,
host of blinking, shifting spots

of blindness at play over the constant
grinding of some machinery
or some other. Fuelled with fluid.

Fluid signatures stroked but not
unsigned, checks not yet
in the mail. As if an armored

peace had settled down
over the torse of the peninsula,
turning the dog's eye and lion's

tongue into silence, breathless.
A sound akin mosaic. Concentration
ardor slips, loses time, pops off

into a premature inhalation.
I anticipate your touch at times
to the bottom of my perplexity.

The crisp and washed expanse
of exurban lawns to flash
by the windows of our muscular

speeding cars. Anticipate crowd-calls
and sullen laptopped, multi-tasked
attention. Concatenation ardor

like tongues of fire burning scales
off eyes or some damned thing.
Whose name has dropped off

my leaking PDA. Lucky PMS.
And kudos to the plucky young ones
who've hacked their way

out of an overcast weekend into
a bright future. If you talk constantly
about money, that means you're all

money's interested in. (Poetry
is a kind of money, but money's
after all a kind of sex. Or vice-versa.)

There's a pylon down the street
to measure incoming airplanes' decibel
levels. Good sounds to me.

The senses variously drawn from line
to dotted line, fences that shelve
us off from our hungry neighbors

who might take away our stuff.
That man wants your money.
So you tripped him up, showed him

which end went where and how many
fingers it really takes to make
a fist, though most punches

these days get lost somewhere in the tubes
and wires of internetted social
space. So much talk of *free will*,

quaint and almost risible relict
of some underdetermined
stone age, when Dad could pop

the hood and tell you why
the engine didn't go. No need
to change the oil of our wondrous

self-lubricating market machine
so long as there's a queue
of dropouts and fuckoffs waiting

to open their veins into a funnel
over the whirring cogs and wheels.
(Getting a bit burned out

on the clockword metaphors,
old son.) One's whole life like
a hunk of dry-cured ham, and yourself

keeps dipping off and changing the soak,
salty as ever. Nothing like a sunny,
breezy afternoon to blow off melancholia,

though: the playground equipment shines
like a wheelbarrow in primary colors,
no splinters from a picnic table

pressed out of recycled plastics. Tenacious
and fiercely territorial ants (*provident
emmet*) will crawl your wrists

and ankles, remind you and your children
that all's not yet petrochemical
culture. He wrote it blind, feeling

the next expansive period
on his pulses, as the subdued noise
and crisping air told him

night from day. The experience
of defeat, a regularly marked
fencepost for the merchants of Utopia—

for whom nothing less than the City
of God, superimposed on Berkeley
or Des Moines, will do. Count

your blessings, girls and boys,
close your eyes and pray, stretch
out on your pallets and think

of *patria*: it's a finical, untrustworthy
dark out there, but then again.
A band of thunderstorms moved east

across swamps pavements and trailer
parks, us thinking only of our individual
leaks. Mosh-pit discourse, where ideas

and invective bounce off one another, come
to rest pressed against the crowd,
sweaty bloody breathing heavily.

But blindman he takes an idea, tumbled
and polished like an amateur's stone, sets
down and follows it inevitable out.

The woods are full of lucky bastards
like that, shuffling behind trees
and peering out of bushes. Enough time,

enough energy, and we'd be there
as well. Two plastic children's slides,
side by said but jaunty out

of parallel: light and shade, a switch
I wish you'd effing stop
flicking: pillows stained with hollow

coughing, the berry-magenta
drip of flavored lozenges.
That particular cough felt something

like a fist, a disconnection notice, final
warning—where's your surrealism now,
as they hustle you into the next room

stifling shocked sobs? Electronic
klaxon, repeating synthesized
and spinning *co-co-rico-co.*

Premising rain. Damp gust, or
money sieving through the smallest
membrane imaginable

into the bloodstream at large.
The body politic shooting up
on petroleum, which you won't see

on the *New Yorker*'s cover. I'd guess
we need a prophet, though I'd
settle for a smiling prophetess

with blue eyes brains
of steel and large soft breasts.
Hyacinth hair, they say, because

of the clust'ring ringlets. Sere remains
of the potted basil by the pool
pump: extension cords laid

over dry ground, ant-crossed
sand, naked to the welkin. A licorice
tin of hobbyist's tumbled stones.

The Book of Meat / Samuel Johnson

Its covers open like a rib-
roast, its spine—well, a spine,
knobbed, bumpy, slick
with fluids. And then,
the lamps:
      Your hair spreads above me
a curtain of night, shadows
generation. The shopping mall
buzzes with fear and commerce,
armed guards threading the ranks
of broad-beamed offroad
vehicles, gleam in the shadows.
Chill of the poured
concrete seat radiates through woolen
skirts, fingers into clenched
thighs. Breaking into form, routine,
      breaking repeated gestures, twitches
      and saccades, sink-a-pace gait
      and touching every post
      of the picket fences—fog
         of mosquitoes, crusted
         sand about the tongue and eyes
         of ruined sneakers
My hand touched the moisture
of your sex in a lightning-flash
of initiation, flower
opening between my fingers
into a salt-sweet lotus, mouthful
of communion bread.
The title *Rambler* a *pis aller*,
last-minute decision—as if
he had not rambled
smoky well-dark

streets, unlighted
by any reeking lamp. The great
    form rolling back and forth,
    blind eye in its orbit, infinite
    sadness of his pawing
    those unseen breasts beneath
        the bedclothes, longing—days
        an endless series of marks
        on paper, scribbles slowly
        fading into noise
The Book of Meat, Its Sources, Uses
and Divine Particularities: to be read
with The Book of Sperm and
The Book of Spattered Blood, by
an oil-soaked, sputtering rushlight;
    (one reads her body's architecture
    and geometries with the eyes
    and practiced metrics of the hands,
    blindly, *feelingly*) one reads those enfolded
        leaves blindly, in the thrash,
        the parted sweetness
        of vegetarian flesh
To say, in the language of play-
acting: take that down, my lord, reach
me the handle of that tousled
water-closet or the trailing edge
of that rolled bumswipe: my angel,
my flying valkyrie, my pink-titted
divining-rod—the mornings fade
into sullen afternoon, the clamp
of your thighs about my skull
pounds a resinous theater
into the caverns behind my eyes.
    Spatters of wind, sparkles
    of warm rain, chasing the fire-
    ants widdershins into their lairs.

§

bend down you fabled aviatrix
mistress of struts fuselage
and yellow busy wasps
beneath your canopy I acquaint
me with sea-surge the moan
of dark and underwater
caves swim through the air
on pinioned and tense wings
lights dim and pattering rain

§

The dawn strafes and reapportions light, and the horizon,
boundless and without form, crawls into a human
cast. We thrashed in fluids and coiled sheets
all the livelong night, sleep descending finally
like a clumsy colophon, afterthought. Key in
the measures of outflow and income, chronic
inequities hanging over bürgerlich lintels.
        There are no ferries in the land without hills,
        insect partitions chipped away at by hands
        calloused and nobly soft. A Kia would
take us there, a Scion, but the system of the world
(impatient, imperative) demands a certain solidity,
gravitas. The reader turns over the pages
of a single book her whole life through, her auditor
cocking his head, rapping the table in the darkness.
        Shadows avaunt, phosphorescent or
        fluorescent manifolds, which only underscore
        the beamish stains on underwear or shirts.
                A cigar, that is, splattered with the green
                and milky ejaculate
                of patronage. I seized your hand,

Jacqueline, stared or started into those eyes.
That every twitch of an abdominal nerve
should exhaust markets, bump praxis back
into theory. He seems
            to have gotten around, to say
            the very least. Halitosis and back hair
            no impediment, admittedly, in the antechambers
of our Beloved Industry, a thousand trademarks
tattoo'd on its limply member.

The daylight strikes and strafes us deaf,
Damascene roadishly. An RSS feed
from deity, astrological signs in the shapes
of electrical fields overlapped in rooms
            of our cathedral-ceiling houses.

§

Twitching under a burden of guilt
            and things undone, unfaced
obligations. I would settle matters,
            make all the blustering papers
to settle in stacks or vanish
            into the shredder. I would see
you gone, the old familiar ache
            almost a comfort. *Barren*
sceptre indeed, limp and
            senseless. The frogs boom
out their staggered chorus
            of desire, fuck-cycles
of beautiful nature, and
            the seasons—having no
alternative—turn their slow,
            painful face, like an aged dog.
The self simpers its most

maudlin, not strip-tease
but exhibitionism, thongs
        and nipples of the heart.

§

If you move someplace out west—
Tucson, say—the tubes and wires
will stretch to breaking,
will break? A white, a comforter,
a soft. Unwarranted resentment
of the word "salad," the words
"snack," "slice." Legs in sheer
black sheaths, hinged pink
and open. Bits to remember
lying in a ditch, face-
down. *The boards
did shrink.* When you write,
do it cruelly and well, teeth
shining, eyes alight. And often.
Altitude and seasons, leafmold
and nosebleed.

§

The clouds swaddle the sky
        —vile metaphor—
like a transitional object, and all
the wee stuffed animals huddle
together in their dripping dens.
The secret life we maintained against
the world's life, an interzone.
Sweat and juice runs down between
your buttocks, fingernails
in my back. *From each according*

to his abilities, says the newscaster,
straight-faced. Rain all day, all
night. Cache of lizard eggs
        laid in a tarpaulin
in the carport, delicate
and white. Freckled breasts.
I would seize this traffic, slow
or stop it by some energy
of mind. Solitary lamp before
your door, flatscreen television
alight. A mirror multiplies
        our coupling. It's true I cry
at the smallest things, a song
on the radio, flash of stocking
and bright hair, bumper sticker
on an unfamiliar car. Rain
        all night. Secret life,
interzone, maintained against
reality. A hole beneath
my lung, fertile aching something
removed while I—unknowing—slept.

Damage Poem

Consider the poem as killing machine, sharpened word-gears
turning word-gears, greased and shining engine-block of
        pornographic
technology—not the catherine-wheel of "genuine" emotion
        rising
from the swamp of tranquil reflection. It twists
the threads of Penelope's loom into knotted elf-locks,
seeds the reader's browser with subversive cookies:
the poem as vicious animal; the poem as
tumor, bulbous and unclipped umbilicus. No more poems
as consolation. I want the poem as damage.

www.ingramcontent.com/pod-product-compliance
Lightning Source LLC
Chambersburg PA
CBHW031929080426
42734CB00007B/612